Eternal Life
and other poems

Eternal Life

and other poems

by
Gene Fendt

First published in the USA
by Angelico Press
© Gene Fendt 2025

All rights reserved

No part of this book may be reproduced or transmitted,
in any form or by any means, without permission.

For information, address:
Angelico Press
169 Monitor St.
Brooklyn, NY 11222
www.angelicopress.com

pbk: 979-8-89280-075-4
cloth: 979-8-89280-076-1

Cover design: Michael Schrauzer

CONTENTS

Valentine from St. Augustine 2

Catechism for Our Time

La Citta Eterna 5
Catechism for our time 7
Short Interview after a Purported Miracle 9
The Original Position 10
Elizabeth 11
The Lyric Frame of Sorrow 12
What my mother saw 14
The magic trick 15
Than teach one star how not to sing 16
Dark Matter 17
The Good Samaritan 18
Analytic of the Sublime 19
Today's Weather: The Parable of Snow 20
Edmond Georges Grandjean 21
Body and Soul 22
Spring, Platte Valley 23
Hiking to Devil's Bridge, and down 24

How it is

The Wing 27
Laundry day 28
Elegy, for my father 29
The Divine Record 31
Requiem (for Don Welch) 32

La Cathédrale 34
Lot's Wife 35
Something in our cells 36
Galapagos: Sea Turtle 37
How it is 38
Six kinds of silence 39
Letter to St. Augustine 41
Act of contrition 43
Dante, to Beatrice in a world that was not his 44

Eternal Life

Report of the anthropologist 47
Walking the Platte 48
Annunciation 49
The Song of Joseph 50
Full of grace 54
Visitation 55
Advent Prayer 56
Christmas Song 58
Orison of the husbanding soul for his bride 59
Elegy in ordinary time 60
Resurrection 61
Unrhyming sonnet for my godchild 62
Eternal Life 63
On the resurrection, against the pagans 64
Agatha, to Quintian… 65
The ecstasy of St. Teresa 66
Hockey in the City of God 67
All Saints' Morning 68
All Souls' Liturgy 69

Anselm's Poem 70
To the virgin of Guadalupe 71
The Longest Jump Shot Ever 72
Walking in the dark 73
After the resurrection 75

Acknowledgements 77

for Don Welch

—river guide, interpreter of birds, gift—

Valentine from St. Augustine

Would that you, far from my only love,
could see my love in you, only to become
the more united to my only love,
which love I love in you.

Catechism for Our Time

La Citta Eterna

L'inglese poeta Giovanni Keats
Mente maravigliosa quanto precoce
mori in questa casa
Li 24 Febraio 1821
Ventisimosesto dell' eta sua

From the plaza above you can see
all the way to St. Peter's and think
that he must have been able at last
to find symbols of all of us here:

The Eternal City around his home
grows older and more decadent;
the smell of decay yellows the dome,
beggars lie by the fountain in rags.

We wait for the angel to stir the waters;
he comes, and who is first to the water
is cured of all of his ills. Some here,
Master, have waited for years.

Above, in the gardens of the Borghese
(the palace closed for three years),
an artesian bubbles into a pool, runs away—
disappearing again under ground.

(The stone sifts its grout through still air,
Daphne, fleeing horrid Apollo,
turns to laurel as his hand grasps her thigh.
Dark dust covers their polished flesh.)

The poet from his window is able
to look on the plaza and hill.
The yellowing dome is invisible,
invisible, too, the pool.

*By the waters of Babylon we sat down,
we hung up our harps, and wept,
in Babylon...* Sing me no more
of the songs of Zion.

Old whores know the night
hides many lost virtues,
lends a negative capability
imagination lacks in daylight.

*

Below the inscription stands
an unstrung lyre
set in modern concrete
where marble once had been.

Catechism for our time

Who made you?
    Desire made me.

Why did Desire make you?
    To know its power,
    to serve it and never be satisfied.

Whence comes this God?
    He is ancient of days;
    his worship first rose in the Land of Want.

What is the kingdom of Desire?
    Time,
    and all of space.

Where is its capital?
    In each heart.

Who is its king?
    No one.

Is this kingdom rich or poor?
    It is very rich. Having one product,
    that it has in infinite supply.

What product has it?
    Despair.

How is despair produced?
    It is eternal, the only begotten
    of desire itself. Whatever desire imports,
    despair is exported; whatever desire exports,
    this it imports.

Is this economy universal?
    It holds only within the kingdom,
    and in each capital.

Does Desire have a temple?
    Many in each capital,
    so, an infinite and ever-growing number.

What are the names of God?
    They are uncountable and various,
    but his people are all one.

What is the name of his people?
    Each one is called Narcissus.

In what does worship consist?
    To drown oneself
    and not to die.

What does God promise?
    Never to answer.

Short Interview after a Purported Miracle
(Jn 11:38–46)

What was it like?
I hardly know. After all,
I was dead.

It's to be expected:
There isn't much to say about
not being.

No; no light—
but neither dark; nor small.

I heard a call.

From nowhere—where I was.

Felt bandages on my head;
came out.

What does that mean—to doubt?

The Original Position
(Rawls, *A Theory of Justice*)*

Under the condition that you know nothing at all,

Under the condition that you are allowed only five
kinds of question and that generally only one will be answered
with any plausibility or degree of accuracy in any specific
                                                               instance,

Under the condition that your mother and father shoot craps
over your as yet unformed face,
with no stricture on their talent, capacity
for raising a catfish, or patience with croup,

Under the condition that no one knows who you are,

Into a world with uncountably more churches
than ever it had active gods,
and more methods of suffering than those purposed
by the most exquisitely appointed of dungeons,

A world where every system of order
is enforced by crucifixion
and the end of each road is death,

To what system of taxation would you like to consent,
and when will you begin paying?

---

* In *A Theory of Justice* John Rawls proposes that in order to produce an equitable social contract, we imagine all members of the society behind a veil of ignorance, where they have no knowledge of themselves or their socio-economic position in whatever society is agreed to from within this original position.

Elizabeth

Elizabeth takes her clothes off for the moon
upon the lake; leaves fall, silent as her dress,
around the maple, and her lover licks
the waves, her arms, the small prayer of each breast;
she lifts the window, night air fills the room,
the subtle light embraces all she is,
embues her sacramental bones with grace,
baptizing in the name of the water, and of the moon,
and of the maple loosing its leaves before her face;
and the light comes into her like a swan's neck
dips into silver water, and going down,
eyes open, she sees her own feet in a world
merely translucent, not yet shot through with love.

The Lyric Frame of Sorrow

"I like your apple pie," he said,
embracing her from behind,
"but I really love your buns."

He leaned into her, his hands
impossibly under her apron, blouse, and bra
as she leaned out to place

the pie up on the cooling rack
beyond the child's sudden hands.
"One of us is going to get burned,"

she said, wishing the signs of his affection
would avail themselves of times
less inopportune, if not, precisely,

dangerous. "We're out of milk,"
she said, blue veins warming in his hands.
"Take Tommy; I'll get the table set."

"And then…?" he murmured in her ear,
one hand trailing down her stomach.
"We'll eat."—She turned and pecked his lip.

*

October and the trees in their celebratory fall
chasuble the hills in martyr red and gold,
bereave the sunset of her glory for a day,

orange the moon, and set the river's curves aflame;
for nothing turns the planets from their courses: the sun
declines from Libra to the Scorpion; the car,

returning, rounds the downhill curve to find the tank truck
stalled. Standing on the brake he pulls his son's head
to his lap, turns right hard, goes under; the car

is opened like a can of Spam. A neighbor runs to the road:
a glittering angel lies in the lap of the headless man,
a bruise above one eye, no further harm; *no further harm.*

What my mother saw

One early Sunday, delivering papers
in streets plowed and packed to ice
that we declared playable—
meaning hockey—and cold enough
to get my mom to drive the route,
I took three hefty *Journals*, hit the houses
across the street, and, never looking,
crossed to her side.
                        A cab shot the gap
between our car and another parked
across from it, and in the mirror
my mother saw her son go down,
the red lights lit, the cab
                        slid like a puck on ice.

I rolled backwards, landed on my feet;
my mother embraced the cabbie:
There is joy, and then there is rejoicing.

That afternoon the puck rose
off my father's stick,
shot up mine, defending,
and whacked me in the forehead.

I went down, saw stars, stopped the game
spread out on the pavement:
Four stitches, small scars,
stopped games, and sudden stars.

The magic trick

The slip-knot holding your strands of years,
winding out of nothing, through all
the changing cells—
hair, nails, skin, desires, fears,

has slipped entirely   off;
the magician's quick trick tells
us all
of measureless void, of total loss,

unwinding sinews, slack strands.
How, in his hand, does it disappear?
Where go? Why? Not clear.
Straight silk, silence, empty hands.

Than teach one star how not to sing

How beautiful the slow burn of autumn,
the fire descending from the tree tops, the sun
rising late, removing itself, its flat light
sharpening each thing's edge, sumac's bright face.
The long rows of rolled alfalfa let darkness
pool along their northern sides—day done in:
the dead corn shows every rib of the fanned field.

So we would wish ourselves to be and go,
but our apple went from flower to blight
in May, two maples, as if with
early Alzheimer's blushed to bare in June.
Our lovely neighbor, four children under eight,
found Lou Gehrig and gurgled all through summer,
leaving too much sky, much more than
when the trees were taken.

Is any creature owed what it has not received?
The longer darknesses hide our loss,
as shallow streetlights the deepening choir of stars.

Dark Matter

From where we are, it looks
like every galaxy
is moving fast away,

and all the stars accelerate
into the dark
that they will leave us in,
spinning, and alone.

I wonder if it's us.

The Good Samaritan
(Rembrandt, 1633)

Hound in foreground, shitting;
horse in center, not.
Ostler's boy holds reins;
ostler's man unloads the horse.

Above, the ostler in the open door,
purse slung beneath a mid-age gut,
listens, near disbelief, to orders
from a richly robed Samaritan.

Fondling himself in public,
unsure except he has empursed
all the surety desire can—
swelling, with promise of more to come.

Analytic of the Sublime

Provided we are in a safe place,
we should like to see ourselves
strapped to the bed of nails
and walked on by the elephant;

provided there is an exit,
we wonder what it is like
to sit
in the plane that is falling,

or be trapped
in the burning towers
as they collapse.

If we knew
the tank would come to a stop,
we too would stand there
free, in our white shirt, before it.

Given the end of the world,
let us watch
in the theater of the gods,
grasping the ticket we don't believe in.

Today's Weather:
The Parable of Snow

It has been falling for hours
in the night—
straight down, great, soft flakes:
the mercy of God.

It clings to rest on every thing,
this cope of grace,
an inch of thick, bright heaven
on each brief twig.

We will make a mess of it
with our engines,
the mess will freeze tonight:
curse it.

Edmond Georges Grandjean
1844–1908

An accomplished painter of horses and contemporary of the impressionists, Grandjean belonged to a different tradition, believing in a meticulous observation of nature and its careful rendering, a procedure he carried out with great technical skill. Since his death, his work has not appeared on the market, primarily because his fondness for large scale compositions limited his output.

Why would a man spend his days so—
not an exhilarating landscape
or a highly accomplished fixer of cloud—
but the meticulous tracery of gas lights,
the crushed slather of horse dung,
the exact railing around the roof,
no surreptitious cloaked figures,
but a well fed porter, waist unbuttoned,
pausing on his horses for a cigarette:
no stunning blues, or green, or yellows,
the sky ready to break on a day heavy with rain.
And foreground—horses, exactly muscled,
their short-napped hides bristling
against girth cinch and bridle,
their shit-stained legs,
brown and inexpressive eyes,
with lashes like a girl's.

Body and Soul

The old truck,
like a fat man in a squeaky couch,
dips deep in the slow road's ruts;

high in the blue,
the hawk.

Spring, Platte Valley

Red capped, the cranes are calling
the sun's love up across the plains;
winter melts back north,
its tale drooping. Amid the chopped stalks
they splay their arms and dance,
these martyrs of desire returned.

Hiking to Devil's Bridge, and down

Spiraling deep maroon beneath gray skin,
the red cedar holds its new fruit
too high for any hand,
its tough low branches broken,
worn to polished knobs;
only the highest are full green.

Sixty years? On the path to Devil's Bridge,
where thousands follow thousands
in every season—even this,
the hottest and most forbidding—
each carrying his own glad water.

Time, impossible in these burning hills,
carinates; the time-bound creature
wears into dust, vapor, almost mirage.
Shadows slip on the steps, an echo
comes from somewhere, like a voice.

The virgin's deep blue mantle swells,
unblemished, over the sanding carnallite.
Four thousand feet below,
alleluias of saguaro run down the hills
to a happy lake, where rushes wait,
bending.

How it is

The Wing
(*Phaedrus* 246 d)

The function of wing is to take
what is heavy and rise with it
to the region above, where the air turns to fire

so cold that one's breath comes out
permanent snow,
and falling to earth sublimates instantly,

or falls
only in fast moving water,
the open-work crystals dragging

impurities down to the mud,
silting the river's edge quietly till spring,
when the sunflowers, cattails, bulrush and gentian

rise up;
and warming, the chrysalis opens
and snow turns again into wing.

Laundry day

The first load was always diapers.
I would hang them in disbelief—
their absolute white against the motley

sky, the color stripped garage, the pathless
grass; folded in thirds, and then in half,
I carried them in against my face:

the breath of April, May, June…,
ready for whatever the lower world
would dump on them.

Elegy, for my father

Nothing we do
is like this. Death makes all
an echo;

no voice remains
original, no act
one's own:

Thank God.
Dying lets fall the good, the bad,
but only one

has form,
can hang for any time
upon a tree,

or band a finger,
or bring the human animal
into grammar,

into answer
out of mewl and oozing pleasure.
So he did

and ceased himself:
diffused into effect:
became a ghost.

*

The day before he died
the late sun turned the bird bath
to a shallow bowl
of molten copper;

burning as it was,
a robin came to it,
dipped, and drank in iridescence—
then froze, bronzed by thirst

and capillary action
of its spindly legs. It held.
One other came;
it drank, then both were gone.

The deep green chain of peonies
held the shining bowl
like a pendant from which, somehow,
the living jewel had fallen.

*

God precedes the world
announcing nothing's nihilation,
leaving behind

the bang of beings,
remaining himself in all of it
and beyond.

But we are not
like this; we do not make
the day,

only shape
the fruit of it, or polish
the skin.

The Divine Record

The shifting tones
are etched in each coronal suture;
the slow bones form

the record, mark
the music spheres' intent surrounding swell
as the skull hardens

and we fall
into the deaf state of meat and bone
and bowel.

Suppose He bless:
Say God's finger trace the flesh freed gravure
long after death,

would not your skull
gather all its bones to hum again
the music you never heard?

Requiem
(for Don Welch)

The voice is no longer a voice,
the man no longer a man.
Before sounding, the voice could not
be measured, and now
it can no longer be measured.

The dust of his voice has been weighed,
sifted and weighed, and placed
on her lap, a plain box:
sixty years of knowledge
and love, eight pounds of ash.

His voice seemed sometimes
to measure itself through silence;
the next word comes when it will,
the world turns, we measure,
still, the white space of silence.

Spring: the river braiding itself
around its sand bars, falling
slowly from the high desert
to lace its meanders into green;
the sky full of wings, ancient and new.

Which of these cranes, mating for life,
might have their syrinx song
modulate to our human voice,
praising sandbar and river and the braid
of love under the descant of cranes?

From which of these welcomes
should a poem be born?
Remind me, as these ashes float
and settle, in what simples
all bliss is borne.

La Cathédrale
(Rodin, 1908)

They could be two hands praying,
but you see they are two right hands
and are not clasped,
but arch and touch—just so.

        Late in afternoon, face west,
        the sun streams through them
        without the colors of Notre Dame,
        but see them from the west, blotched and gray:
        They could be two hands praying.

You see they arch and touch
just here and here,
and frame an empty space—
They could be two hands praying.

Lot's Wife

Sodom must not have been perfect in evil.
Not, at least, to Lot's wife, who could remember
days washed in sunshine, setting the clothes to dry
on prickly pear and eucalyptus,
talking to her neighbor with the sweet
clean smell rising around them.
Quotidian work, oblivious of evil,
too ordinary to be of note
to God, or Abraham, or Lot.

Knowing that, she lacked the one virtue
needed for decisiveness in life:
Don't look back. The thought of what you lose
would turn anyone to stone.

Something in our cells

Something in our cells remembers Paradise:
the sweet sapped trees, the flowering grass,
Eve's immortal flesh ecstatic entering Adam's
under the boughs of the tree.
Something in our cells retains
the honey God brought from the hive,
the bees cloaking him in a human shape,
the honey running down the chins
of those two, sweetening all of our flesh
to all of our days, so still there is
something in our cells.

Something in our cells remembers happiness
and seeks it everywhere,
as souls, they say, seek God,
or moths the distant stars.
Something in our cells recalls
the morning of eternity
and makes us hear in all our happiness
something else—
some unbearable singing
of something in our cells.

Galapagos:
Sea Turtle

On an island of bird calls and ever crashing surf,
collected shatterments of whelk, starfish, conch,
a shipwreck built upon the back of centuries of coral,
green by accident of wind and promiscuous gull,
I woke and walked. My bare foot kicked up
a curve of marble skull cup, smooth
as any goddess' flesh under Praxiteles' hand,
its soft parts worn away, its outer shell still gnarled
and mottled like the sea. How did it happen
to this one? What day, what season, what sudden tide
making toward this island flipped it backward
against the sharp rocks of the headland, or forced it
tight between two stones—its short limbs pawing
wildly in the merciless air?
Or had its ancient slow metabolism ebbed,
and the aged turtle crawled across the sand
to where its mate last housed their egg,
a delicate shell enclosing the next century's life,
and there, as we will, not without pain, turned
to give its thanks for life's fine high play
which turtled over us and leaves
love's strange, rich-vaulted shell
to wash up on the shore and there be found
by some early rising beachcomber, alone,
in a misty foreign dawn, long after we have turned
to water?

How it is

Before the beginning was the now
and beginning began because of now,
and from now, and in now.
And there was no before, before now,
and after it is only time,
and after time there will be
only now.

Then every private sunlit now,
and each separate fog-shrouded April now,
and every mutual, *oh my love, now* now
will be folded into that eternal now
and be at once and always now.

And though in time there is no time
for now,
and though all time folds out
the now,
divides and subdivides and shatters
now,
hangs up, drags out, puts off
the now,

all time, still, depends on now,
and can suddenly, at any moment,
break wide open
into
now.

Six kinds of silence

There are six kinds of silence,
and three of reticence;
noise is all of one kind.

The names of silence have never been known;
reticence does not speak its name.
The name of noise is: noise.

Noise reverberates outward;
silence carries its echoes within.
Reticence has no echoes,
but it allows the echoes of silence
to rest in its most intimate center.

No kind of silence has a history,
but every true story leads to one of them.
Reticence allows true stories to unfold
like warm air licks open April's
multifoliate rose. Loud facts
cannot endure such genuflexions.

The echoes of silence are distinct
in tone, key, and timbre. Reverberation
is mere prolificness of sound.

Silence is the hollow body of a woodwind,
reticence is the reed.
Music is the breath of reticence
through silence, into our common air.

Noise increases the density of silence
until it becomes unbearable.
If silence reached critical mass
the world would explode of its weight.
Reticence allows silence its voice,
and so the world continues.

Death is a silence that does not know itself.
Love is a silence that does.

Letter to St. Augustine

Excellency,
             I have no questions for you,
only for me, but since they raised themselves
while listening to your sermons, or reading
your *Confessions, De Trinitate, Enchiridion*,
I write to you; you needn't answer, I know
your days are busy, ground to dust, to darkness
with the thousand things a bishop has to do
before he can retire for a moment—
to pray, to write, to think about a book.

But I wonder, if love's our weight,
are there people who are weightless? I don't ask
to judge my brother, but there are times I wonder
of myself, I seem so purely pulled
to nothing. Now, for instance: I ask,
but don't await an answer; do not, in fact,
expect it, but dream of wide free spaces, floating
like the gull on wide-winged air—
effortlessly.

You say that God could not allow
any kind of evil in his works
unless he were so powerful, so good,
as to be able to turn all evil,
finally, to good, and so reveal
the weight of sin is grace, its gravity
a sign: *res et sacramentum gloriae*.
I cannot doubt this, only wonder.

I wonder, too, if when our souls are finally turned
to face that ever warming fire, if from our ashes
there might rise some new and unimagined way
of loving, some way we know not of, nor guess,
until whatever we are now has reached
the other side of fire, and life, and mercy's justice,
embodied and immortal, lives as it will.

Such are my meditations, such my prayer,
and so this letter, from many thousand miles,
near as many years, to you from your brother,
deep in the bowels of the good God's body—

Act of contrition

Like that nameless woman who carried
the sweet perfume of her sins
within the translucent jewelled egg—
large as an infant's head—
itself a lover's payment,
my soul does not desire that you
should take her up, but only
to break upon your feet, and seep
like oil into your holy flesh, O Christ.

**Dante, to Beatrice
in a world that was not his**

The accidental photo from our wedding
catches us together, turned to smile
at the unknown taker. A small spotlight
above my head shines into the hall behind,
still darker than the room we're in.
Behind you, a candelabra's score of lights
fits you like a crown, pushed back a bit
because my head is tilted in:

Remember me when you come into the kingdom.

Eternal Life

Report of the anthropologist

There were two tribes in that country:
One had no rituals; the other did.
The people of the first tribe
breathed, ate, procreated,
and so continued their kind.

The people of the second tribe
engaged in the daily rituals
of breath and heartbeat,
digestion and procreation.
What it meant is lost.

Walking the Platte

if you would see the shape of things to come,
study the blackbirds:
their gleaming ebony flight
drafting the wind on silent wings

if you would be wise, become like the river:
desiring neither shore,
nor the ocean to which it goes:
its swift rippling stands in place, the water moves

if you would have hope, you must bend lower:
feel how tendril roots of prairie grass
hold grains of sand together against wind and water,
and doing so, go green

Annunciation

Without turning she knew the voice
which, kneeling, asked if she would condescend
to let the world turn its wobble-axised grief
      through her unentered womb:
allow the tears of children and of Eve
gather in one place, dry land appear,
Word grow to globe, named things,
      that smash-skulled Abel open
his flowering brainpan to the murderous brother,
knowing all, allowing all, that forgiveness
      make its round of all,
from the god-draped temple of her flesh
to the last star, speeding in its red shift
      from heaven's center.
All of which, including this visitation,
would be, only if she already had said yes.

And God grew humble at her affirmation;
obediently, he childed himself to her obedience,
and love became human, and dwelt among us.

The Song of Joseph

Joseph you have heard
What Mary says occurred;
Yes, it may be so.
Is it likely? No.
  —W. H. Auden, *For the Time Being*

We met when she was twelve, and I was twice her age,
but two—that was not unusual then—and she
drew from me a wish that now seems very strange:
      love is always moved to the impossible,
and gives what it most needs to whom it loves, unneeding.

What I wished—no unusual dream—was to protect her...
So two years later we engaged: she'd be fifteen,
her parents approved; she did not reject me,
      but gave the look that made her age-mates still:
not questioning, but calm: *what do you mean*

asking to do what God approves, or imagining
that we this moment are from his view or ever hope
or wish it so? Mornings at the well she'd sing,
      but when the sun beat in the loins and loosed the tongues
of pleasure-seeking girls, her arms would lever up

a sweeter water, and her eyes above the water
made them wonder what led their mouths to lick the dust.
Did I think, without me, some evil might have caught her?
      Did I imagine, manless, she'd be unfulfilled?
Dry and weary, they eat earth who consider thus.

Before our marriage she found herself with child.
No one was shocked save me, for she would bring her work
and sit with me, and people think what people will.
       Uncomprehending, she wondered that I could be
                                      non-plussed:
was there something I didn't know? could there be hurt

in what she carried? Can lovers' questions start with how?
Where there is love there is the deed before intention.
Perhaps I wavered. The angel asked if she looked now
       at all less full of grace, and bade me hold my tongue.
I did; and took a pregnant wife. Let me mention

how my arms loved to hold her growing womb; weeping,
I would kiss her there, and now I can desire
no other intimacy, no other earthly sweetness,
       no other words than these, which must be sung,
and are, by creatures made entirely of fire,

eternal, lit by love for her, though born in time—
but I exceed my understanding. She carried him;
they were given to me, or I to them... In fine,
       Augustus, on the Feast of the Unconquered Sun,
ordered each to sleep in his ancestral home.

We travelled slowly, for Mary and the child's sake,
through a slow rain, the roads sloppy with mud and dung,
lights out, inns closed, their keepers surly at the gate;
       despairing, I brought Mary to the door; the man
apologized, brought his wife to us. When it was done,

she brought us swaddling clothes, and so another subject
was born into the Empire's scheme, the world of death
and taxes—the binding unsought chances love must accept
      in every age. Then the miracles began.
Kings came. They'd traveled months, crossed deserts on a quest

for something which, until they came, had not existed,
meeting us where, had we our will, we would not be.
Another dream, 3 a.m., not to be resisted:
      Get up now: wake Mary; go. She woke, bundled the child;
the ass was not recalcitrant, headed for the sea.

I followed her. The news behind us was not good.
We turned into the bloody sunset, went west
to Egypt along the coast. Everyone knew. Food
      was given us, fodder for the ass. Arab guile
lost itself in kindness, shared its fire; coins pressed

themselves into my hands, and strangers, turning off,
thanked us for travelling with their tents. We stayed four years.
To Nazareth returned, the common yearning of
      simple people bound by geography and weather:
rain, sun, a cooling breeze, balm for every child's tears—

Nothing extra-ordinary. No clay birds
brought to life, no healings of a playmate's cuts,
no cabinets finished while I slept. He stirred
      honey in his milk like every other child.
We traveled once; Jerusalem homes made huts

of Nazareth. The temple put our synagogue
to shame. I could buy a rabbit for what I paid
for two small sparrows. Expensive business, praising God.
      Jesus met his city cousins—a little wild—
he had his mother's look, and calmed them down. We stayed

a few days more than we could well afford,
and leaving, hurried; left the boy behind. Two nights later
we were rushing back to each related door—
      vainly. Mary, truly anxious, wept aloud.
That shook me. No access of grief would sate her.

I bought two sparrows; then we heard our prodigal's voice
within the rabbis' courtyard. With her own look
he stopped his mother's sorrow, rushing in. Rejoice:
      for the dead return to life, and what was lost is found,
two sparrows bought for sacrifice were loosed.

The teachers had not slept for three days running.
Nor had we. Nor Jesus. How we were to know
he would be there I have not the cunning
      to suggest; forgetting it was Mary's deepest wound:
but ignorance is endless, therefore love is so.

Amen. That is my history; this all I know.

                                    Patmos, July 1996

Full of grace

already he was united to her,
already she knew him through himself
already he was seeing all,
though he had made it,
through her virgin eyes

so, having come to see, he asked,
would she consent that he become
himself, apart from her: a sword
cut through her heart, but love said yes
and so he came to be a part

of all she saw in seeing all
through him, her virgin eyes
still pure mirrors of his making.
She appears, they say, even
to those who know her not, or fail,

uncognizant of herself, while there
before her, wondering where she came from.
So Juan, and Bernadette, Jacinta,
and other shepherds first,
nameless, whom happy we would be

Visitation

Mary, I dreamed of you last night,
      or someone who spoke of you, full of grace;
And when you called from the road
      the child came alive in my womb.
And Mary, you know this fig tree hasn't flowered
      in over twenty years, but today
I woke from my dream and it was covered with blossoms.
      They have quivered all morning with bees
Who cannot resist their sweetness; the courtyard is full
      of the smell of creation, Mary, in six months
We shall have enough figs to feed the whole village.
      And look, Mary, my long unsuckled breasts hold milk!
And before these blossoms fall my nipples will be as figs
      in the mouth of my child. I have waited for this so long
That I had forgotten that I *wanted* it to happen.
      Now it has and my husband is dumb with disbelief,
And I have more words than two tongues can utter.
      Mary, what great thing is happening?

Advent Prayer

Let me hide beneath your cloak, O blessed mother,
that Christ, coming, may take me for his brother.

There are so many dirty windows in this church.
How much smoke in its age?
How many guttering flames?

How could one ever get high enough to clean
the apse ears,
or find the toothbrush power to polish
the carmine bits
without punching them through the loosening lead?
or cracking the great blue cloak
of the long ago virgin?

    Rejoice, O highly favored one!

And the outside—another age
of boom and bustling weathers—
farm dust, sanding sleet, the baked dirt
of other people's waste and work.

And all that birdmire on the ledges.
Decades of sitting on the edge
of getting in:
Going and not going;
pecking at the growing shadow.

    How may this be done?

Hunger has an inside, and an out:
When the doors are shut, silence fills,
but does not swallow:
Accept the Lamb, then taste.

O Queen of heaven, rejoice!

And with the darkness heaven sifts its snow;
the world whitens, each window's edge
accepts its softer ridge,
remits as praise the moon's
expectant light, rising from the new blanket.

Now, and at the hour

Christmas Song

Tell me now, you angels of the Lord,
how heaven's gates were opened by God's love,
despite the barricade where we piled each great
and meanest thing, and leaned on them, and leaned
our weight against each other, our weight,
and all the earth we said we loved, not knowing love,
because one woman's heart allowed
her own humiliation, and the bastard
son of God her womb. Tell me how many
millions perished, waiting how many thousand years,
for one slim girl's abject acceptance,
which none of us can fathom still. Tell me
how love lives, though all our hearts despise it,
and divinity is houseled in an animal's stall.

Orison of the husbanding soul for his bride

Let this kiss be for your waking mind a door to love
the only door to the only world made and waiting

Let this kiss and this open your eyes
to the made world waiting and lovely for you,
the instinctual I drawn through these eyes to its face

Let this kiss enlarge under your breast
till the kiss is the shape of your heart,
and one with it beats in the world till its end
in the world without end which it opens to kiss

Let this kiss over your womb proleptically bless
all children everywhere yet to be born
and all of us rest—babes in arms, wizened,
full grown and dead, adolescently dense,
untrained or untrainable, precocious and mute

Let this kiss be thanks for the sweet and the rich
smooth flesh of pears, passion fruit, apples
in their syrup of sun, all animal loins,
all gravies and spice, butter fresh from the churn,
sweet onion, wine, lotus and rose

And this kiss and this descend on your weakness
and history's blood, accidents, botched
operations, uneven deliverance, inadequate loaves
that these knees never buckle, lock rigid, or fold:
Let all live on only in love

In this kiss and this on the soles of your feet
be my sins remembered, trod on, tread out
and all of your prayers all alive all rejoicing

Amen. Alleluia.

Elegy in ordinary time

When the undertaker comes, tell him
a plain pine box rough joined
is all I want. I will not be
the death of cherry, oak, or walnut,
finely lacquered; save such work
for dining rooms, your unborn daughter's
jewelry box, the bedroom cabinet
of my only love, whose white fingers
rest on its satin finish, lightly,
just after brushing the hair my fingers' bones
will put on flesh again to run through.

Tell him so. And if he balks,
then burn me boxless;
let the earth in me become itself
through fire. And fired, white and grey,
distribute my ashes to them all--
whoever comes: a pinch to sift
like lint through their pockets, a teaspoonful
to mulch their garden, globe to fruit,
a Lenten thumbprint to mark
themselves with, begging grace,
and when, years hence, you weep
at Eucharist, know the dust,
the very dust of me achieves the wheat,
and we are won, and one.

Resurrection

μη μου απτου, ουπω γαρ αναβεβηκα προς τον πατερα
—Jn 20:17

    Though now we are less light
    than inward curving heat:
    insufficient, dying,
    clinging to our dying,

    On our easter this flesh
    will gather like a star
    and all the light we could not be
    will not stay within.

    That day we shall embrace—
    this buried love arise
    the handiwork of God.

Unrhyming sonnet for my godchild

This childish spell, so long as it enfolds you,
has no need for miracles, for all
that is is wondrous—that there are mothers,
that they come when you cry, that crying
ends, and leaves no memory, that blankets
are tents, and tablecloths, and curtain: peek-
a-boo! and good is everything, and bad
falls a way like a full diaper, and you
go naked through the living room. This spell
will one day end, and leave no memory,
but you will know it must have been,
and words like these will be your only key
to that warm room whose door is shut behind you,
like love before you knew the word, like hope.

Eternal life

*Eternity is the complete, simultaneous and perfect
possession of everlasting life; this will be clear from
a comparison with creatures that exist in time.*
               —Boethius, *Consolation of Philosophy*

In a way of living which leaves no room for time
the seed, the bud, the flower are all one present.

It is too much life for this poor rose,
which needs it parceled out in petal moments,

glorying in each: its own slow climb,
in sun, in moon calm rain; all earth's elements

driving through its thorn as blood goes
round the body, carrying the blush

of love some time, of fever, or delight—
as a child on a slide in one great flow

swoops down, shrieks, runs back to climb:
all, all at once is life, there is no rush.

Can all this, alive, as one day's raiment,
be borne forever up in one man's bones?

On the resurrection, against the pagans
(Augustine, *City of God* 22.11)

Varro says a vestal virgin once,
declared unchaste, took water from the Tiber,
carried it in a sieve to pour upon the altar
—proving thus her chastity intact.

Doubting not his learned source, Augustine
translates the pagan miracle thus:
The weight of water held in air by virgin trust
proves that earth—now full of living spirits

bound to earth—may rise in us to live and
move in unaccustomed ways through air, stone,
river, what you will. What tiring god or demon,
lately left for Christ and resurrection,

held that weight of water 'gainst a nature
we think we know, could scarcely be so great
as he who made the stars, gave all things weight,
and keeps immortal spirits quick in sluggish flesh.

Doubt not then, pagans, your ancient tales true
foretell much greater acts our God will do.

Agatha, to Quintian,
    consul to Decius Trajanus, Emperor
    from prison, February, anno Domini 251

There is, my love, no garden save our God;
why, then, do you complain the world does not content you?
or think to take your pleasure and your ease
upon my breasts? It is not love if I should let you

rest there, or pillow where my stomach rises
from the cleft where you have lost yourself—
or wish to—our God does not allow it:
Imperial marriage makes me a part of all your wealth

though lady of it; to your joy I shall
refuse it. No sacrament of love attempts
such transubstantiations. Your hands must offer otherwise,
else, to you, these breasts are prisons, deaths, contempts.

Seek not the plausible unions of your mortal will,
but love impossibly, or kill.

The ecstasy of St. Teresa
(Bernini, 1652)

Hands limp, her eyes roll back into her skull,
and all her nerves' ends fuse open
like fine wires under a soldering gun,
go silver and set, her heaven hallowing
come-cry echoes out like beaten gold,
her body becomes reverberate heat,
pure energy, the marble, shimmering illusion—
the cooling backlit dust of a cosmic explosion,
the heat fixed negative of film—
angel and angelic arrow fall away,
her long-limbed bliss melts through the grasping rocks
like Proteus, like a tide rising infinitely
outward of its own accord, pulled
by no distant planet: a wash of ecstasy,
a love without purpose, a letting go.

Hockey in the City of God

"the body, better than it was here in its best estate of health"
—Augustine, *City of God* 13.20

Unlike the lake and river now,
where crack, stick, snow patch,
tread-melt trip and slow
the skate blade, will you watch

the cicatrice on the dustless mirror
heal itself behind you? Ice gleam
as if untouched but for
the wind which swept it clean

of snow, banking the river
that perfect day you found it once,
a glorious Thanksgiving,
on the bend just out of town?

Or rather will nature be itself
renewed? To friction give its scar;
the body, its best estate of health
surpassed, from which not its power

but all need is taken, balanced,
singing on the blades; and action:
you wheel, slinging the puck
off the stick's curved face, willing
time true, and each his own perfection.

All Saints' Morning

The world woke wearing white,
the last gold leaves bent slightly
on the trees, the fallen open
their drier arms, dead kites

accepting air's last gift.
The road, a black river, frozen—
as each gutter-gathered denizen
accepts its new white shift.

All Souls' Liturgy

At all souls' mass, suddenly,
each one's wounds opened:

mother, brother, deepest friend,
husband, sister, child—

unraveled bandages
fell: ravened, agape;

their quick still roiling,
they calmly stood

rent through to their creation.
How breathe? How live?

How left here so?
Our Lady's chapel's windows

dawn behind them;
equable and sure,

their limpid gazes wait,
resting on the reader:

The souls of the just
are in the hand of God.

Anselm's Poem

Wishing to paint a picture, each selects
something substantial which to paint upon,
for no one paints in water or on air.
            —Boso, in *Cur Deus Homo?*

Open now what is impossible:
God's omnipotence everywhere enthroned:
for out of nothing, in no thing, blue heaven
appears; darkens to reveal its own
depth of endless stars, and here, a mantis
praying on the rosebud twig. All instant
with the Word who is eternal wisdom.

Why then in God-made man does God himself
one time come to dwell? *Cur deus homo?*
Vying with himself to turn our evil
out of his creation? Come there by our choice
is He? Our happy fault a cause to him?

No. How then should this be understood?
Ordering justice reconciles to justice
ordered through obedience, which is
but gratitude, clinging to the giver
through all his gifts until the end—not ending.

To the virgin of Guadalupe

Because you said there shall be roses,
there are roses blooming in the snow.

Because you wished the faithful poor
to be believed, your image wrapped its arms
around him, and his cloak became cathedral.

Because your perfect body only
always bent to your own sinless will,
earth's heaven henceforth wears your cloak's color

and honors, by its act, God's poem:
that word become flesh, and body, undestroyed,
put on perfection like a cloak.

The Longest Jump Shot Ever

From out of bounds,
behind the line of history,
before beginnings, without walls,
or floor, or overarching rafters,
bleachers, box seats, SRO
filled to the cheering ceiling,
God launched his Hail Mary,
holy, unbelievable shot:
lights lit, the black line
dropped behind it, boards ran out,
rafters sprang to roof them
and all the audience stood
on the sphere among spheres,
the living ball among incandescent bulbs,
to watch the ball in its high arc
curve around the edge of darkness,
hang, as they hung, curve
in its descent, nothing but air,
and back-lit black space
and then, so suddenly, the orange rim,
the black line,
and nothing but net, curling
on the backspun globe
where all were cheering.

Walking in the dark

"Where are we?"
But it was dark and there was no answer,
only the sound of water lapping just beyond,
lulling, allowing her question
to hold its shape in the warm air—
the question now gathered around her
as the world gathers, as the warm air,
as the dark, and the water lapping.

She seemed to feel the heavy boughs
of great oaks passing above,
which, in the day, would have her
walking in a dappled shade,
careful of roots, but here
the ground was even, almost
unnoticed by her light shod soles.
Still, the breath of such great trees
seemed consubstantial with her own;
her question and the trees breath
the shape and substance of the warm air
she walked in, and the lapping rhythm,
slower than her walk and ever near:
Ahead? Behind?

*

"Where am I?" she thought again,
and the moon rose slowly on her left;
she saw the pathway spring up
across the lake—no sea, no savor of salt,
the moon's brickwork immediate
and perfect on the small waves—
a beckoning. She paused, enthralled:
Not the moon? An open door?
The briefest smile seemed to pass within.

Home? As in Assisi once, she had seen
a great home's sunlit courtyard
from the darkness of a covered road,
and a fountain heard, invisible.
How she had wanted to walk in…
Could she go there, even now?
She stepped onto the path of light.

*

There is a lake you cannot see across,
a forest of great oaks nearby.
There are no footprints in the soft earth;
the moon is just the moon.
He is not there, nor she;
nor can your heart imagine
what you watch, or see.

After the resurrection

After the resurrection
    the breath to play the flute will still expire with the note,
        and all the music of mortality will be recalled in constancy,
reminding us of this time when we are not;

and after the resurrection
    the brute beauty of the kestrel's flight will be its own glory
                                  (as even now it is),
    but we will see our seeing of its glory (our glory),
as now we do not.

The slight service of what one can but does not do,
    of what one knows but will not will,
        will breathe its breath, and then, poor praise,
begin to breathe

Acknowledgements

Many of these poems have been published elsewhere at various times. Thanks to the following for previous publication:

Anglican Theological Review: Annunciation, Christmas Song, Something in our cells, To the Virgin of Guadalupe, Resurrection.

California Quarterly: Visitation.

Christianity and Literature: After the Resurrection.

Hurakan: Report of the anthropologist.

Ithaca Lit: Lyric Frame of Sorrow.

Journal of Modern Poetry: Dark Matter.

Magna Polonia (Krakow, Poland): Agatha, to Quintian; Catechism for our time; trans. to Polish by Anna Szyda.

Midwest Quarterly Review: Elizabeth.

National Poetry Competition Winners 1997: Galapagos: Sea Turtle.

Nebraska English and Language Arts Review: Walking the Platte.

Nebraska Life: Laundry Day; Spring, Platte Valley; The Parable of Snow.

Nebraska Review: What my mother saw.

Nimrod: Edmond Georges Grandjean, La Citta Eterna.

Plainsongs: The Longest Jump Shot Ever.

Platte Valley Review: The Wing, Walking the Platte.

Princemere Poetry Prize: Hockey in the City of God.

Puerto del Sol: Unrhyming sonnet for my godchild.

St. Austin Review: Advent Prayer, Analytic of the Sublime, Catechism for our time, Visitation.

Theology Today: Agatha, to Quintian; Catechism for our time; Christmas Song; Letter to St. Augustine; Lot's Wife; Rodin (1908); Today's Weather: The Parable of Snow; Visitation.

West Nebraska Catholic: All Souls' Liturgy.

*

I would like to thank Matt Duffy for his help in editing this book.

www.ingramcontent.com/pod-product-compliance
Lightning Source LLC
LaVergne TN
LVHW011429080426
835512LV00005B/335